Thank You

# The Farmer's Cart:

## Learning ar words

C. Rivers

# Dedication:

To my husband, Josh. All
your hard work on the farm made
you the incredible father, husband and
person you are today.

"Cock-a- doodle- doo"

The farm alarm went off as the sun started to rise.

And little pig slept
through the alarm.

The farm truck was parked at the end of the farm. But where was the cart?

Carly was helping the farmer find his cart. No luck.

Did the sheep move the cart from the farm to the barn?

Apples
potatoes
onions

Carly walked far to the barn.

The barn looked dark.

Baaah. Baaah.

I saw the cow in the cart.
The cow was going to the park.

The park was very far from the farm.

The farmer was holding a rake in his arm. He was ready to put the hay in his cart.

We saw the farmer's cart.

Far from the barn.

We saw the cow in the cart far past the barn.

Baaah. Baaah.

Let's start a search party
and find the cart.

Carly found the cart.

"Cock-a- doodle- doo"

alarm

arm farmer

far

farm

barn

start

www.ingramcontent.com/pod-product-compliance
Lightning Source LLC
LaVergne TN
LVHW071228160826
845679LV00003B/931
*9798365823570*